1-2-3 DRAW CARTOON CARS

A step-by-step guide

by Steve Barr

Peel Productions

Columbus NC

To my friends, Jeff Parker and Myra Bowyer, whose smiles, kindness, and laughter have given me many wonderful memories.

— SB

Published by Peel Productions, Inc.
Manufactured by STONE SAPPHIRE/LF PRODUCTS PTE LTD, China
Printed September 2011 in Shanghai, China

Library of Congress Cataloging-in-Publication Data

Barr, Steve, 1958-
  1-2-3 draw cartoon cars : a step-by-step guide / by Steve Barr.
     p. cm. -- (1-2-3 draw)
  ISBN 0-939217-75-9 (sewn pbk. : alk. paper)
  1. Automobiles in art--Juvenile literature. 2. Drawing--Technique--Juvenile literature. I. Title: Cartoon cars. II. Title: One-two-three draw cartoon cars. III. Title. IV. Series.

NC825.A8B37 2005
741.5--dc22

2011-0000125787

Table of Contents

Before you begin

Stop! Look! Listen!

You will need:

1 a sharpened pencil
2 paper
3 an eraser
4 a pencil sharpener
5 colored pencils, markers, or crayons
6 a comfortable place to sit and draw
7 a good light source so you can see what you're doing!

Ready! Set! Let's draw!

NO RULES!

There is no right or wrong way to draw a cartoon because there are NO RULES in cartooning. Your cartoon cars can be square or round. The tires can be tiny or huge. You can even turn a cartoon car into a living character if you want!

Don't get discouraged if your drawings don't turn out perfect the first time. That's what erasers are for. If your sketches look different than the ones in this book, that's okay! It just means you are beginning to develop a cartooning style of your own.

Sketch, doodle, and play!

The more you practice, the better you will become. Experiment with each drawing. If my directions tell you to sketch an oval, and you feel like drawing a triangle, draw a triangle! It's your drawing, so you can make it look however you want it. The crazier, the better! Cartooning is all about having fun.

A few cartooning tips

1 Draw lightly at first—SKETCH so you can erase extra lines in the final drawing.

2 Practice, practice, practice! Your cartoons will get funnier.

3 Have fun drawing cartoons! If you think you messed up, just erase and change your art to make it better.

Basic shapes and lines

Here are samples of the various lines and shapes you will use in this book.

Oval

Circle

Egg

Triangle

Rectangle

Square

Boxes (Cubes)

Straight lines

Curved lines

Squiggly lines

Note: It's okay if your shapes and lines aren't perfect, because there are NO RULES in cartooning. However, professional cartoonists sometimes use tools to help them get their drawings just right. If you want a perfect circle, trace around something circular. Use a ruler to draw a really straight line.

How professional cartoonists work

Most professional cartoonists start with an idea in their heads, then try to put it on paper. It usually doesn't end up looking exactly like the original idea. That's okay, because a professional cartoonist can tweak it and fix things as the drawing develops.

I begin by sketching basic shapes, lightly, on a clean sheet of paper. As the drawing begins to look the way I want it to, I gently erases any extra sketch lines. Then I use a black pen to trace over the pencil lines that will remain in the final drawing. Once the inked drawing is ready to go, I add color.

You don't need a pen to finish your final drawing. Just darken the final lines with pencil. Practicing with pencil drawings is a great way to begin to learn. Once your pencil sketches get really good, you might want to try experimenting with a pen to improve your cartoons even more.

Steve Barr

Silly car

You can make cartoon cars any shape you want. Let's start with a silly car with a silly shape.

1 Lightly sketch a hot dog shape. Draw a large curved line on the top of the hot dog.

2 Add curved lines for the windows. Draw circles for tires.

3 Add an oval for the headlight. Draw curved lines for bumpers.

4 Look at the headlight. Add curved lines inside to turn it into an eye. Draw straight lines for the door. Sketch curved lines for the taillight.

5 Look at the final drawing. Erase extra lines. Darken the final lines. Add color.

Now that is one SILLY looking car!

Sedan (side view)

There are several different ways to begin drawing cartoon cars. One way is to use basic shapes as guides, then add lines to form the shape of an automobile. Let's draw a cartoon car using this technique.

1 Lightly sketch a long rectangle for the body of the car. Sketch another rectangle for the top of the car. Notice it is taller, but not as wide as the bottom one.

2 Draw curved lines, inside the rectangles, to form the shape of the car.

3 Add curved lines for windows and wheel wells.

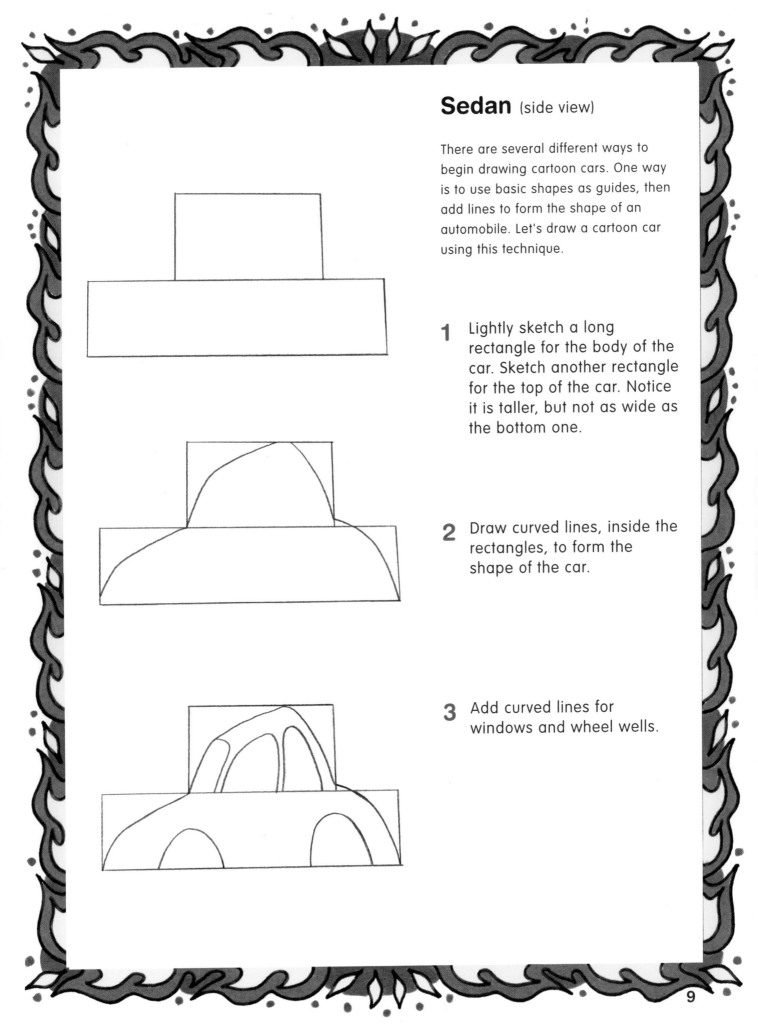

4 Draw a small curved line and a straight line for the mirror. Add straight lines for the headlight and taillight. Draw two ovals for each tire.

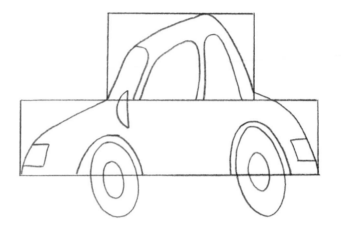

5 Look closely at the driver. Using curved lines and ovals, draw the driver and steering wheel.

6 Look at the final drawing. Gently erase extra lines. Boldly trace over the final lines. Add color.

Cool cartoon car!

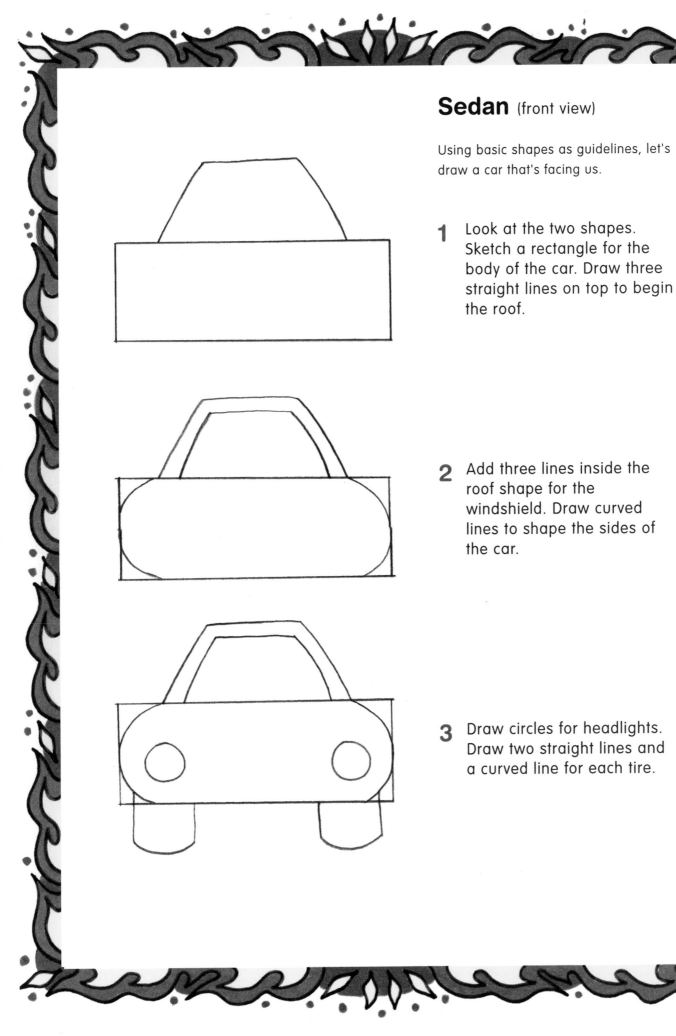

Sedan (front view)

Using basic shapes as guidelines, let's draw a car that's facing us.

1 Look at the two shapes. Sketch a rectangle for the body of the car. Draw three straight lines on top to begin the roof.

2 Add three lines inside the roof shape for the windshield. Draw curved lines to shape the sides of the car.

3 Draw circles for headlights. Draw two straight lines and a curved line for each tire.

4 Add two straight lines next to each headlight. Draw two long straight lines to begin the bumper. Add curved lines on each end to round it off.

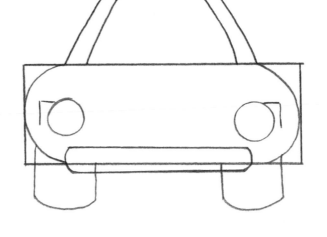

5 Look at the shape of the grill. Using straight lines, draw it. Add a rectangle in the center of the bumper for a license plate.

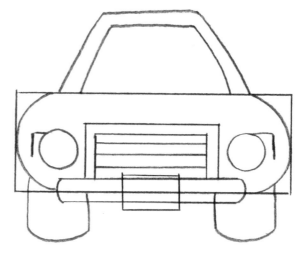

6 Look at the final drawing. Erase extra lines. Bring your car to life by drawing a smiling face in the windshield! Darken the final lines. Add color.

Look out! Your cartoon car is headed straight at you!

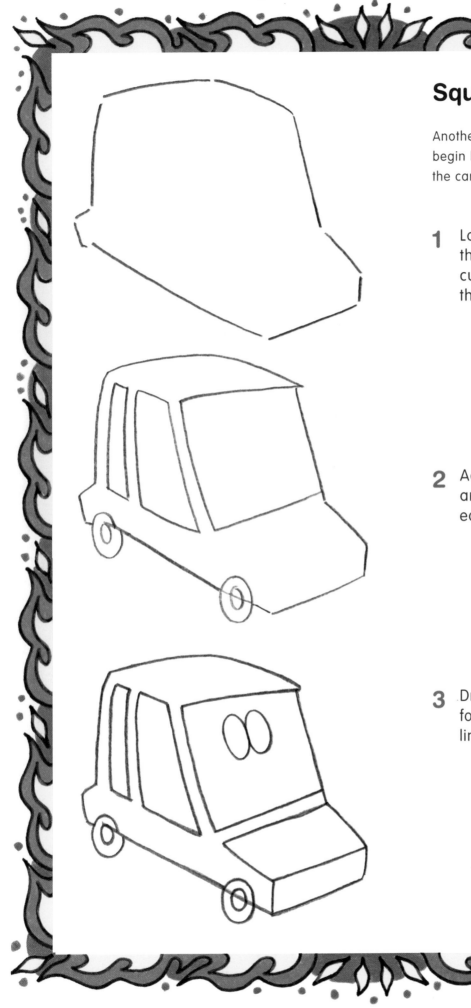

Square car

Another way to start a drawing is to begin by sketching the basic outline of the car. Let's give that technique a try!

1 Look closely at the outline of the car. Using straight and curved lines, lightly sketch the shape you see.

2 Add lines for windows. Draw an oval inside an oval for each tire.

3 Draw ovals on the windshield for eyes. Add three straight lines for the hood.

13

4 Add small ovals for eyeballs. Darken part of each. Draw a curved line under the eyes for a mouth.

5 Add a small curved line on the end of the mouth for a pudgy cheek. Add a long curved line for a big smile. Draw small rectangles for headlights.

6 Look at the final drawing. Erase extra, overlapping lines. Darken the final lines. Add color.

Super square car! It doesn't look like a real car, but that's okay. Remember, NO RULES! It's a cartoon.

Adding faces

You can give your cartoon car a distinct personality, or feeling, by drawing a face in the windshield. Using simple shapes and lines, you can change your car's mood by changing the facial expression.

Here are some step-by-step examples. Try drawing the faces below, then create a facial expression of your own.

Compact car

Compact cars don't have a lot of windows or detail, so they're perfect to draw when you're just starting. Let's draw one!

1 Sketch a rectangle for the body. Add a long curved line to begin the top of the car.

2 Look at the top. Using curved and straight lines, draw it. Add a curved line inside the rectangle for the hood of the car. Add a short, straight line on the back for the trunk.

3 Look at the headlights. Using straight and curved lines, draw them. Add three straight lines to shape the body.

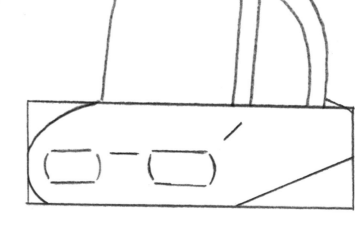

4 Look closely at the wheels. Draw curved lines for the tires and wheel wells.

5 Look closely at the face. Draw the expression you see.

6 Look at the final drawing. Erase extra lines. Darken the final lines to make them bolder. Add color.

Happy car! Bright personality!

Dressing your car

You can add even more personality to your car by adding clothing.

1 Lightly sketch the outline of the compact car again.

2 See the hat shape on top. Using curved lines, lightly sketch it. Draw a squiggly line, in the bottom of the windshield, to begin the mouth.

3 Look at the overlapping brim of the hat. Add curved lines to make it. Draw partial ovals for eyes. Add a short, straight line at each end of the mouth.

4 Add a curved line on the end of the hat brim. Add curved lines for eyeballs.

5 Look at the details on the hat. Use curved lines to shape the top of the hat. Draw a curved line and a small circle inside the hat. Add dotted lines to the brim for stitching.

6 Look at the final drawing. Erase extra lines. Boldly darken the final lines. Add color.

Take me out to the ball game!

Another silly car
(back view)

Let's draw a car at a different angle, one driving away from us.

1 Sketch a long rectangle for the body. Add circles for wheels.

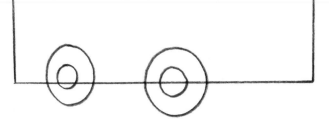

2 Look at the shape of the body. Use straight and curved lines to draw the body.

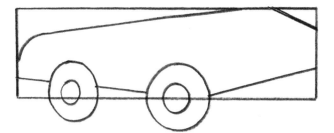

3 Draw a huge curved line for the roof. Add curved lines to the body for a door.

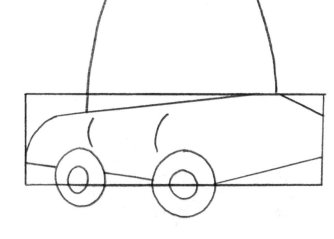

4 Add two straight lines to shape the roof and make a window. Add two straight lines to make the trunk.

5 Draw rectangles for the front and back bumpers, a door handle, and rear lights.

6 Look at the final drawing. Erase extra lines. Darken the final lines and add color.

This car needs a driver. Let's draw one in the next lesson.

Add a driver

Let's add a driver to the car you just drew.

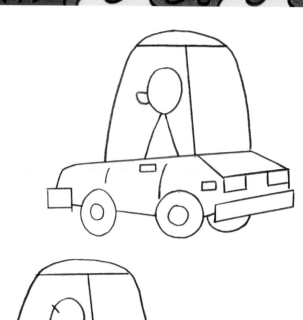

1   Lightly sketch the compact car again, or use the one you already drew. Draw an oval for the driver's head. Add the nose. Draw two straight lines to begin the body.

2   Add the eyebrow and eye. Draw two straight lines for the arm. Add curved lines for the hand.

3   Draw the hair and mouth. Add the steering wheel.

4   Darken the final lines. Add color.

Good driver!

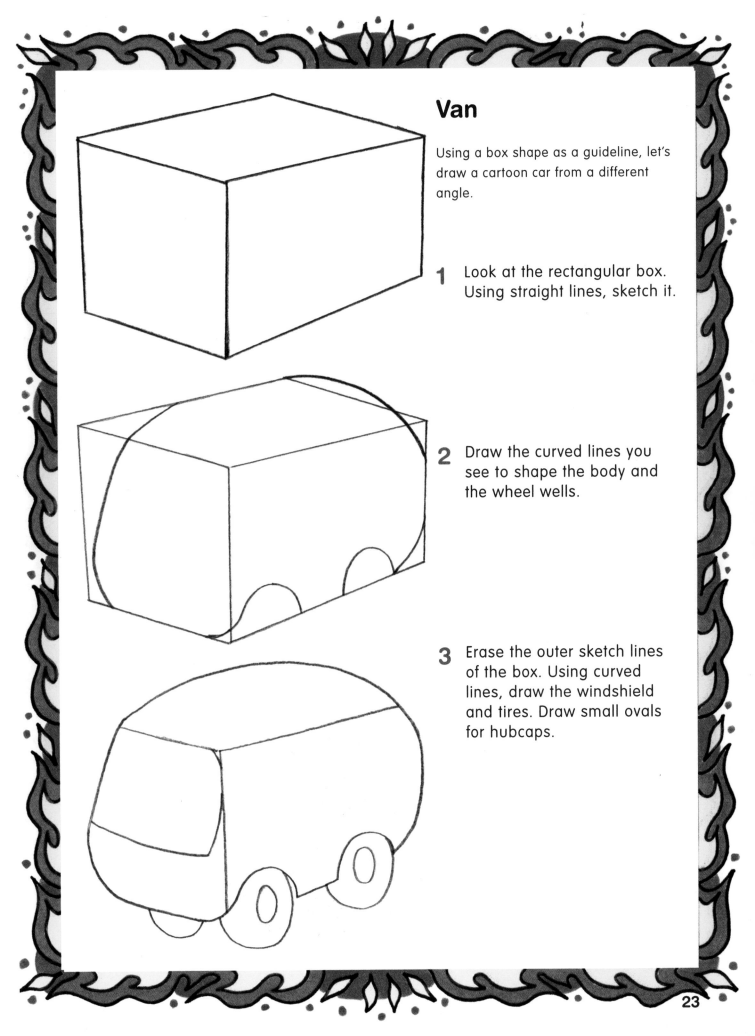

Van

Using a box shape as a guideline, let's draw a cartoon car from a different angle.

1 Look at the rectangular box. Using straight lines, sketch it.

2 Draw the curved lines you see to shape the body and the wheel wells.

3 Erase the outer sketch lines of the box. Using curved lines, draw the windshield and tires. Draw small ovals for hubcaps.

4 Starting at the top, draw the eyes and mouth. Using curved lines, add the side windows. Draw the headlights. Add lines for detail on the body.

5 Draw curved lines for eyeballs and eyelashes. Add curved lines inside the mouth for teeth and a tongue.

6 Look at the final drawing. Erase extra lines. Darken the final lines. Color your van.

Wow! That's one SWEET van.

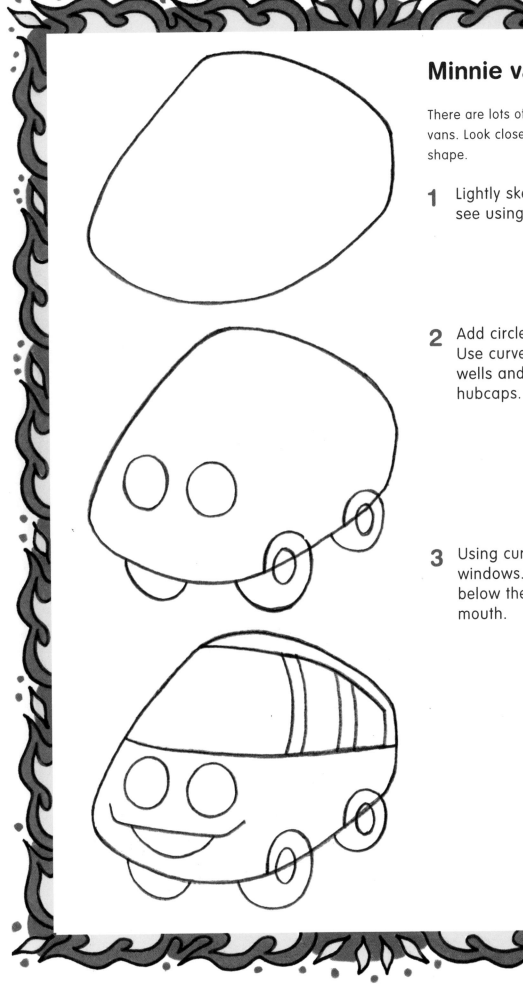

Minnie van

There are lots of different ways to draw vans. Look closely at the beginning shape.

1 Lightly sketch the shape you see using curved lines.

2 Add circles for headlights. Use curved lines for wheel wells and tires. Add ovals for hubcaps.

3 Using curved lines, draw the windows. Add curved lines below the headlights for the mouth.

4 Draw long, curved lines for windshield wipers. Add small circles for eyeballs. Darken part of each. Add curved lines to the body.

5 Add curved lines to give the windshield wipers more shape. Draw short, straight lines for eyelashes.

6 Erase any extra lines. Darken the final lines. Add color.

Cute "Minnie" van!

Changing expressions

You can drastically change a "Minnie" van's appearance by changing the facial expression. Look at these different faces. Practice drawing them.

Sketch the van again. Look in the mirror and make a funny face. Now, draw your funny face on the van.

Go cart

Go carts are fun to drive and a lot of fun to draw.

1 Look at the lines that form the three shapes. Starting at the top, lightly sketch the helmet. Add two straight lines to begin the driver's body. Draw curved lines for the go cart.

2 Look at the shape of the four tires. Draw these. Draw a small circle for the front wheel's hubcap. Add a curved line for the back hubcap.

3 Draw lines on the helmet for a visor and racing stripes. Draw an oval in the center of the hood. Add curved and straight lines to the go cart's body.

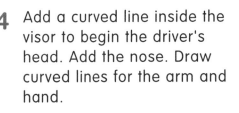

4 Add a curved line inside the visor to begin the driver's head. Add the nose. Draw curved lines for the arm and hand.

5 Look at that happy face. Add curved lines for the eyebrows and mouth. Draw curved lines for the steering wheel.

6 Look at the final drawing. Erase extra sketch lines. Darken the final lines. Add color.

Get ready! Get set! Go!

Station wagon

Station wagons are fun to draw because of their long box look.

1 Look at the long rectangle shapes. Sketch a long rectangle on top of an even longer one.

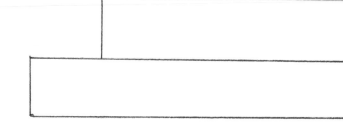

2 Draw curved lines to begin the basic shape of the station wagon body.

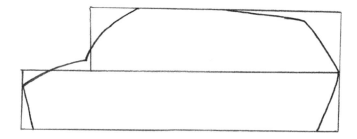

3 Using curved lines, add windows and wheel wells.

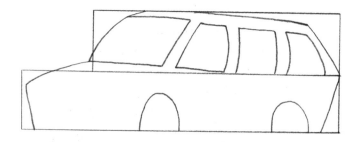

4 Look at the headlights and front bumper. Draw the lines you see. Look at the way the tires are tilted. Draw the four tires.

5 Look carefully at the additional details. Add the lines and shapes you see.

6 Look at the final drawing. Erase extra sketch lines. Add a cartoon face inside the windshield. Darken the final lines. Add color.

Let's add little, curved lines around the tires to make them appear to be moving. Adding long, curved lines behind the station wagon will make it look like it's flying down the road.

Antique car

Antique cars look majestic and they make great noises when they putter down the road. Let's draw an old car.

1 Look closely at the body shape. Using straight lines, sketch it.

2 Add long curved lines to shape the roof. Look at the bumper and wheel wells. Using straight and curved lines, draw these.

3 Add curved lines to form the windows. Draw curved lines and ovals for the tires and hubcaps.

4 Add a line to begin the radiator. Using curved lines, draw the headlights and the other front wheel well. Add a rear taillight.

5 Look closely at the steaming radiator. Draw it. Add additional details you see.

6 Draw a face in the windshield. Erase extra sketch lines. Darken the final lines. Add color

Wow! Classy car!

Grand Prix race car

(front view)

Let's draw a race car that looks like it's driving, right off the page, toward us!

1. Look closely at the shapes in the first drawing. Using straight and curved lines, lightly sketch the two shapes you see.

2. Add a curved line on top to begin the driver's helmet. Look at the angle of the big front wheels. Using curved lines, draw the wheels. Add an oval and a curved line in the center to give the race car shape.

3. Look at the shape of the stabilizer above the driver's helmet. Draw it. Add curved lines for a visor in the helmet. Add a curved line for a windshield.

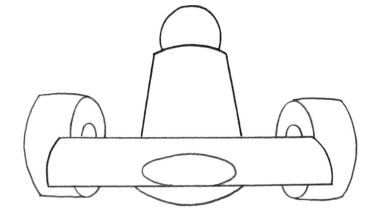

4 Using straight and curved lines, add the rear wheels.

5 Starting at the top, draw the triangle shape on the helmet. Add the eyes. Draw a long triangle in the center of the car.

6 Look at the final drawing. Erase extra sketch lines. Darken the final lines. Add color and some action lines to make the car look like it is roaring down the track!

Dragster

Dragsters race down a straight track at amazing speeds, going so fast that a parachute pops out of the back to slow them down after they cross the finish line. Let's draw a dragster!

1 Look at the beginning shape. Sketch a long, straight line with a curved line at the end, to begin the body.

2 Add a long curving line to complete the body shape.

3 Draw two circles for the back tire. Using curved lines, add the driver's compartment. Draw small circles for the front tire.

4 Starting at the top, draw the head rest. Look at the exhaust pipe lines. Draw these.

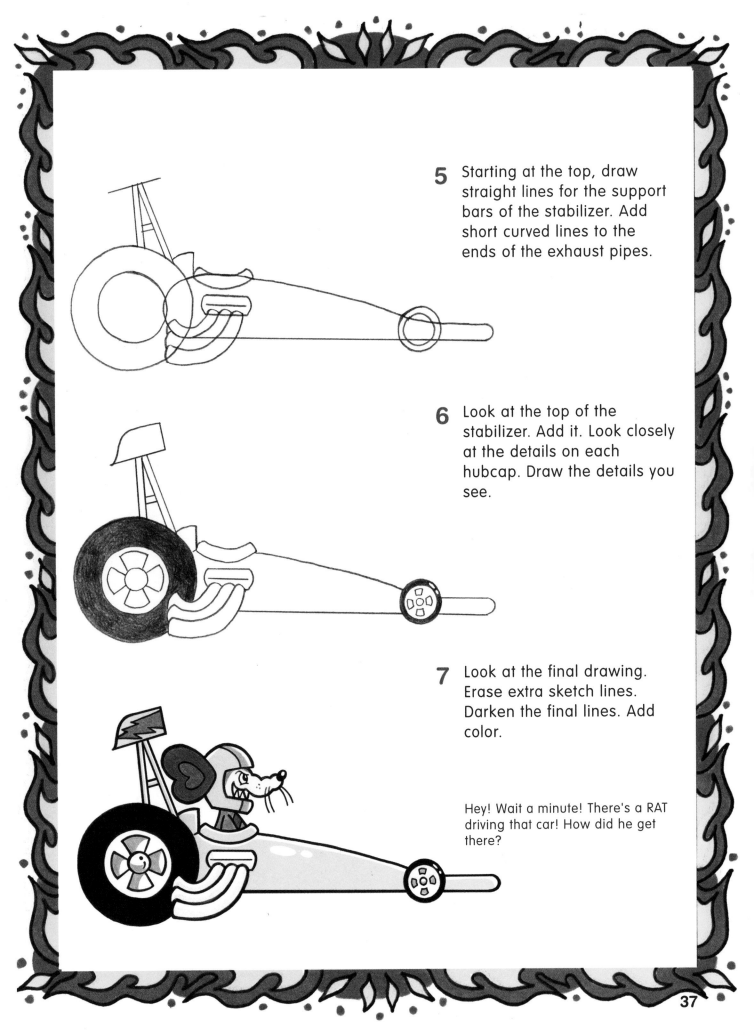

5 Starting at the top, draw straight lines for the support bars of the stabilizer. Add short curved lines to the ends of the exhaust pipes.

6 Look at the top of the stabilizer. Add it. Look closely at the details on each hubcap. Draw the details you see.

7 Look at the final drawing. Erase extra sketch lines. Darken the final lines. Add color.

Hey! Wait a minute! There's a RAT driving that car! How did he get there?

Rat racer

Let's add a rat racer to your dragster.

1 Look closely at the head shapes. Sketch the helmet shape. Add straight lines, under it, for the rat's upper body.

2 Draw curved lines for the visor. Add curved lines to the body for the top of the arm.

3 Look at the heart shaped ear. Using curved lines, draw it. Draw a curved line inside the visor to begin the face.

4 Add a smaller heart shape in the center of the ear. Draw an oval for the eye.

5 Draw curved lines on the helmet. Using squiggly lines, add the nose.

6 Using ovals, add the eyeball and nose. Darken part of each. Draw two straight lines on his chest.

7 Let's make him look mean. Add a curved line at the top and bottom of his eye. Draw his big mouth and teeth. Add curved lines for whiskers.

8 Erase extra lines. Darken your final lines. Add color.

Cool cartoon rat!

Draw another dragster, next to the one you already drew, and you can have a RAT RACE!

Dragster
(racing)

You can use lines behind your cartoon car to show its movement. Or, another way to make your car look like it's moving is to bend it slightly and lift the front wheels off the ground.

1 Look closely at the body shape. Using long, curved lines sketch the body.

2 Add a helmet on top. Draw circles for front wheels. Using curved lines and ovals, add the back tires.

3 Add curved lines inside the helmet for the visor. Draw the curved exhaust pipes.

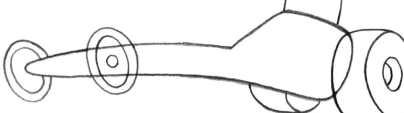

4 Look at the stabilizer shapes. Using straight and curved lines, draw it. Look at the shapes that form the engine. Add these.

5 Add a straight line inside the visor. Draw the big eyes. Look closely at the air intake blower on top of the engine. Draw it.

6 Look at the final drawing. Erase extra sketch lines. Darken the final lines. Add color.

That's one fast dragster, hopping off the starting line!

Sports coupe

Coupes are streamlined to help create the least amount of wind resistance when the car is driving down the road. They have long curving lines to their bodies, and are really fun to drive and draw.

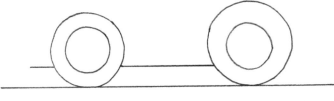

1 Look closely at the size of each wheel and the distance between them. Draw circles for the wheel and tires. Connect them with a straight line.

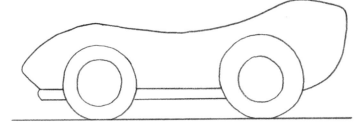

2 Look at the curved body shape. Using straight and curved lines, draw it.

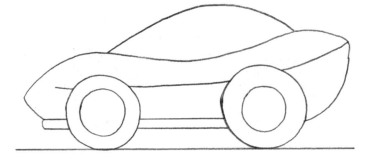

3 Draw a curved line for the roof. Add a curved line in the center of the body.

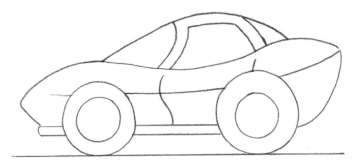

4 Add curved lines for windows. Draw curved lines for the door.

5 Starting at the top, draw a cartoon face in the windshield. Add ovals for a headlight and a taillight.

6 Look at the final drawing. Erase extra lines. Darken the final lines. Add color.

Super coupe!

Squad car

You can change the sports coupe you just drew into a cool squad car by adding a few extra details.

1   Draw the sports coupe again. (See instructions on pages 42-43.) Look closely at the details on the squad car. Using short, straight lines, draw the badge on the door. Carefully add lettering below the badge to spell "POLICE." Look closely at the hubcaps. Draw these.

2   Starting at the top, add the lights. Using curved lines draw an oversized air intake on the hood.

3   Look at the final drawing. Darken your final lines. Add color.

If you ever see a squad car that looks like that behind you, pull over. There's no way you're going to outrun it!

Convertible

Tooling down the road in a convertible, with the roof down, is great fun! Let's draw one.

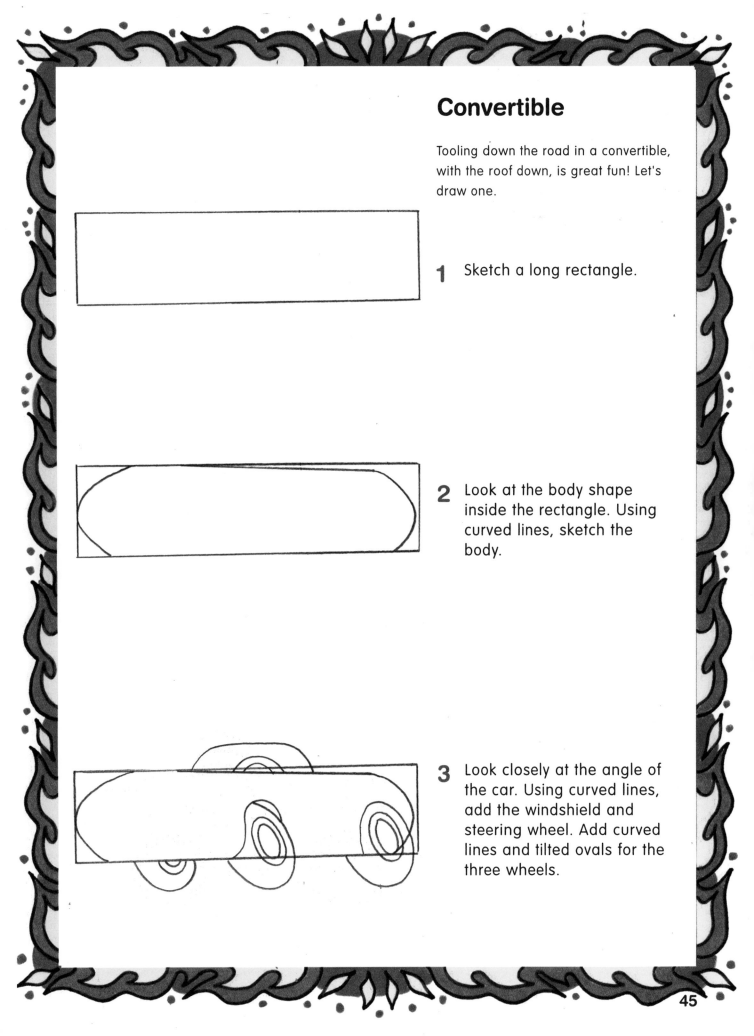

1 Sketch a long rectangle.

2 Look at the body shape inside the rectangle. Using curved lines, sketch the body.

3 Look closely at the angle of the car. Using curved lines, add the windshield and steering wheel. Add curved lines and tilted ovals for the three wheels.

4 Look at the curved lines on the body and hood. Add these.

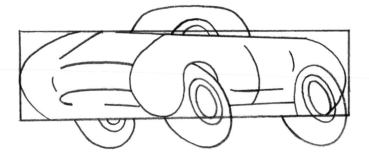

5 Draw ovals for headlights. Add eyeballs to turn them into eyes. Look at the hubcaps. Add the details you see.

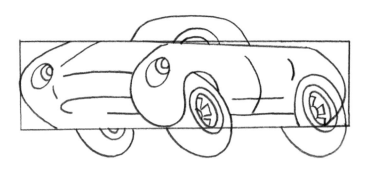

6 Look at the final drawing. Erase extra sketch lines. Darken the final lines. Add color.

Cool convertible!

Dog driver

Dogs love flying down the road, with their ears flapping in the wind. Let's draw a dog driving a convertible!

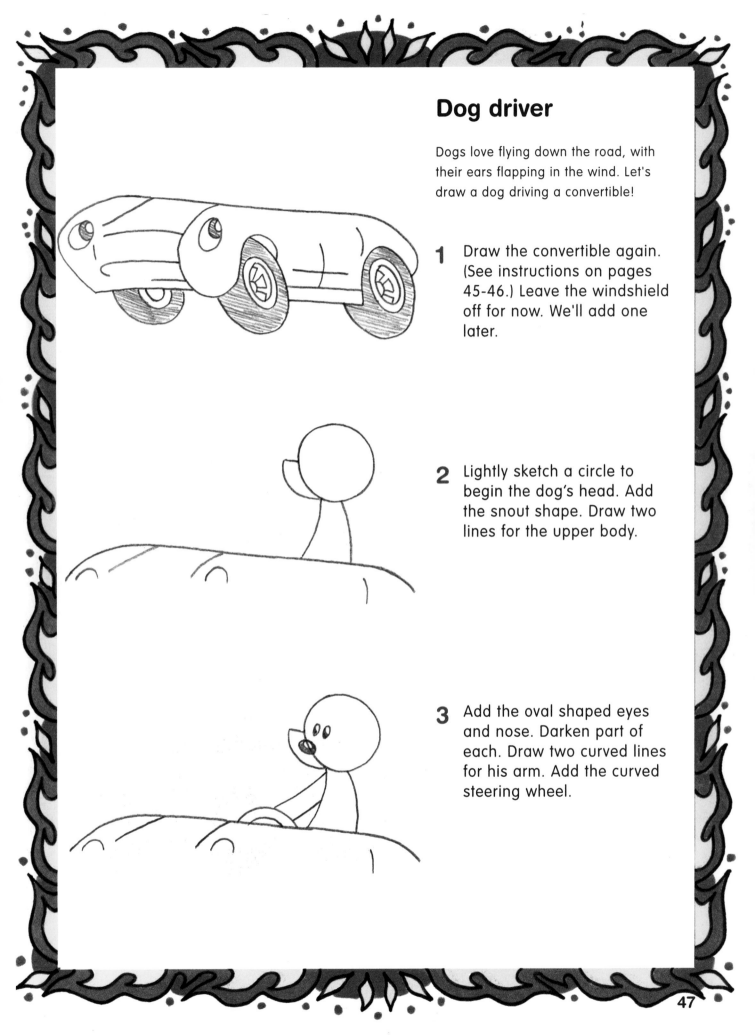

1   Draw the convertible again. (See instructions on pages 45-46.) Leave the windshield off for now. We'll add one later.

2   Lightly sketch a circle to begin the dog's head. Add the snout shape. Draw two lines for the upper body.

3   Add the oval shaped eyes and nose. Darken part of each. Draw two curved lines for his arm. Add the curved steering wheel.

4 Draw curved finger lines on the steering wheel. Add two curved lines to begin the other arm.

5 Starting at the top, add the two little, wild hairs and the long, flapping ears. Draw the eyebrows and mouth. Add fingers to his left paw. Using a long, curved line, add the windshield.

6 Look at the final drawing. Erase extra sketch lines. Darken the final lines. Add color.

Now that's a doggoned happy driver!

Race car

Let's draw a mean racing machine, ready to roar down the track.

1 Look at the two beginning body shapes. Using curved lines, sketch these.

2 Look at the shape of the wheels and the rear wheel well. Using ovals, curved, and straight lines, draw these.

3 Add curved and straight lines for windows. Draw curved lines on the body above the wheels.

4 Starting at the top, add a spoiler to the back. Look closely at the hood shape and details. Using curved lines, add these.

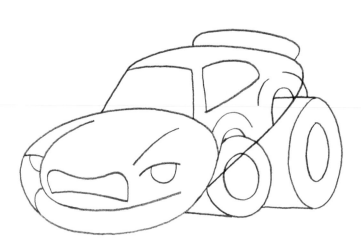

5 Look at the headlights and grill. Add the details you see. Nice teeth!

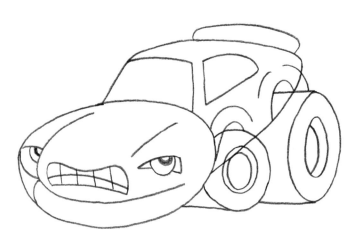

6 Look at the final drawing. Erase extra lines. Darken the final lines. Add color.

Wow! That's one MEAN racing machine!

Souped-up roadster

Let's draw another mean racing machine. If you draw it on the same page as the race car, they can battle it out on the track together. (See instructions for Race car on pages 49-50.)

1 First sketch a long rectangle. Look closely at the four wheel shapes. Sketch ovals and curved lines for wheels.

2 Look at the body lines inside the rectangle. Using curved lines, draw these.

3 Look closely at the roof, window, and engine lines. Draw these lines. Now, look at the tire lines. Add these.

4 Starting at the top, add the air intake. Using curved and straight lines, add the rear bumper, body lines, and front grill.

5 Look at the additional details. Starting at the top, add the details you see.

6 Look at the final drawing. Erase extra sketch lines. Darken the final lines. Add shading and color.

Now that's a car that's going to take off and never look back!

Sprint car

Sprint Cars are amazing machines that fly around a dirt track at incredible speeds. They don't have windshields, just protective nets. The drivers wear disposable visors on their helmets and throw them away when they get covered with dirt!

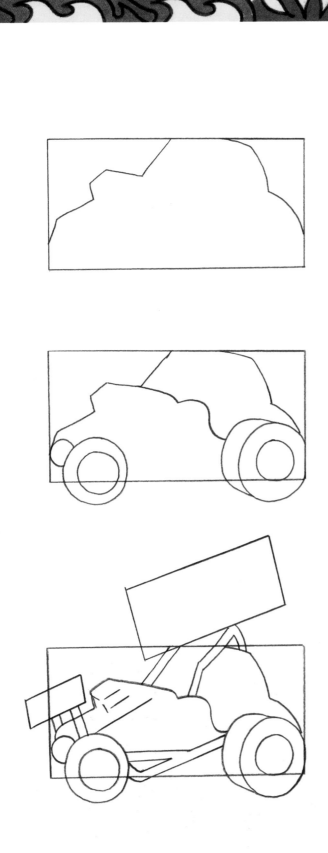

1 First sketch a large rectangle. Look at the outline of the body. Draw these lines inside the rectangle shape.

2 Add ovals and circles for tires. Draw a small circle for a headlight. Add curved lines to the body shape.

3 Look closely, top to bottom, at the additional parts. Draw rectangles for the two stabilizer wings. Add the pipes and hood lines.

4 Look again at additional details. Add these. (Sprint cars are actually push started by another car, so they need braces on the back.)

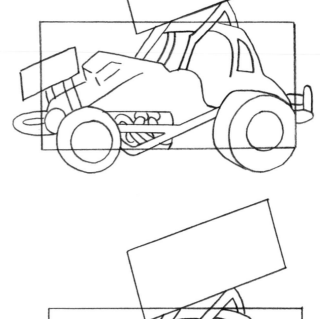

5 Using curved lines, add the protective net. Draw the driver's helmet and body.

6 Look at the final drawing. Erase extra lines. Darken the remaining lines. Add your name, number, and extra details you see. Add color.

Kevin Drury's sprint car moves so fast, it's hard to even draw it!

Stock car

Stock car racing is one of the most popular sports in the world. Millions of race fans flock to NASCAR events every year. Even more fans and drivers go to smaller tracks each weekend to participate in stock car races. Let's draw a cartoon stock car!

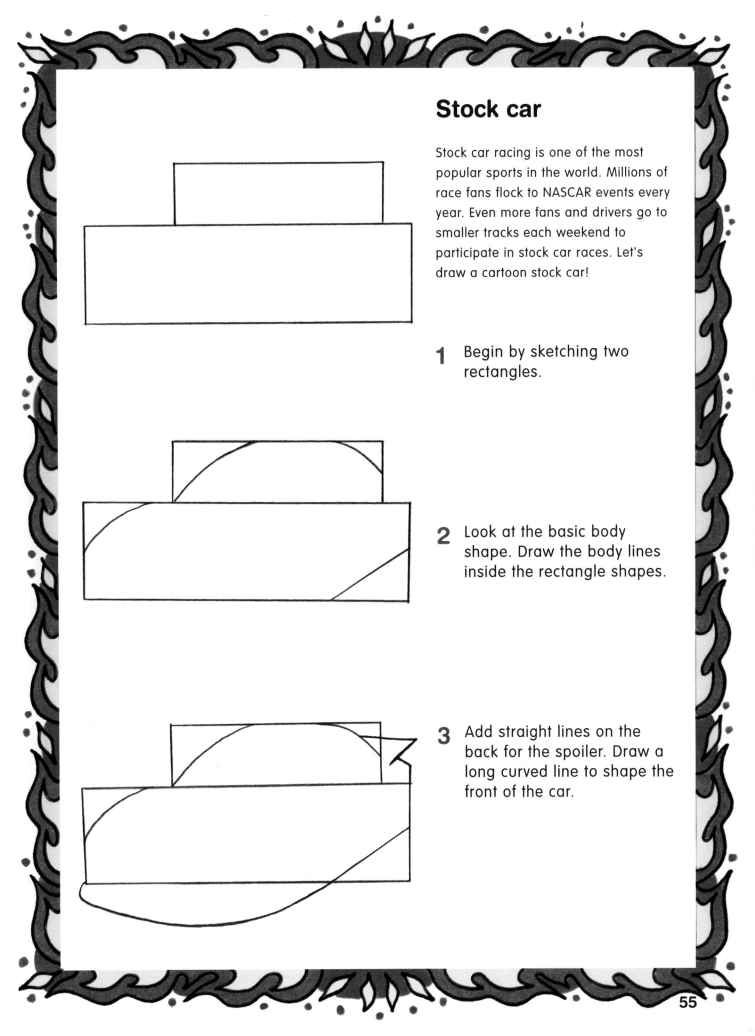

1 Begin by sketching two rectangles.

2 Look at the basic body shape. Draw the body lines inside the rectangle shapes.

3 Add straight lines on the back for the spoiler. Draw a long curved line to shape the front of the car.

4 Erase the extra rectangle sketch lines so you just have the body shape remaining.

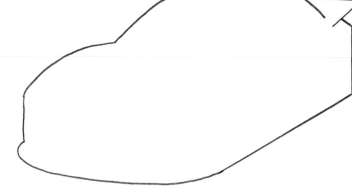

5 Draw curved lines for the windshield and side window. Add a long curved line for the bumper. Draw curved lines for wheel wells.

6 Draw curved lines to define the hood. Add a straight line on the side of the car and a curved line above the wheel well.

7 Look closely at the additional details. Draw a small rectangle for a mirror. Add ovals and curved lines for tires. Draw the headlights.

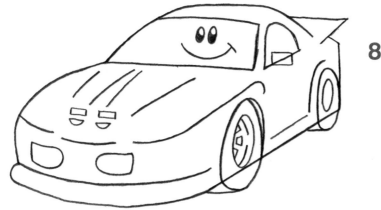

8 Draw a smiling face in the windshield. Add the hood scoop. Draw the hubcap.

9 Look at the final drawing. Erase extra lines. Darken the final lines. Add different shapes for sponsor's stickers. Draw a number. Color your car.

I wish I owned stock in a stock car! I'd probably be rich. If not, maybe I'd get to drive one around the track a few times.

Bring your stock car to life!

You can make your cartoon cars even more human by adding arms and hands. Arms and hands on a car? Of course! It will bring your stock car to life.

1   Draw a stock car again. (See instructions on pages 55-57.) Draw curved lines for arms. Add ovals on the end of each arm for hands.

2   Add curved lines for fingers.

3   Erase extra lines. Darken the final lines. Add color.

Bravo! Number 1 won.

Volkswagen bug

A Volkswagen Beetle was my favorite car. It was painted bright yellow and had denim seat covers. The back seat even had a denim pocket sewn onto it. Let's draw it!

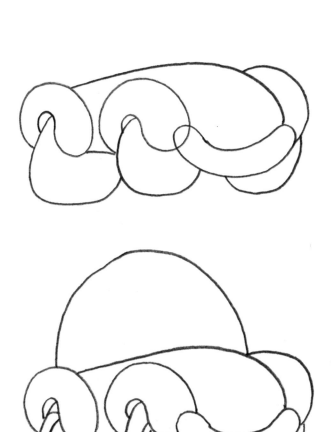

1 Look closely at all those curved lines that form the basic "Bug" body shape. Draw these.

2 Draw a long curved line for the roof. Using curved lines, add detail to the tires.

3 Draw curved lines for windows. Add curved lines and two small circles to the hood.

4 Look at the seats and steering wheel. Add these.

5 Draw the radio antenna. Add the headlights. Don't forget the eyeballs.

6 Look at the final drawing. Erase the extra lines. Darken the remaining lines. Add color.

WOW! You are a talented cartoonist!

Add enhancements

Draw roads or tracks under your cars to accent the action. Add sound effects by adding big letters above your cars for the sounds they are making.

This convertible is roaring down the road. Try writing sounds for your car's engine winding out or the tires burning rubber on the track.

Have fun!

Sketch, doodle, and play! Let your imagination run wild. Let your drawing hand go crazy and see what comes out of the end of your pencil!

Experiment with different shapes and lines. Try combining different parts of the cars you drew in this book to make an original cartoon car. Create your own car. Exaggerate details.

Keep playing. Create more art that is uniquely your own. Sign and date all of your drawings. Save them in a folder.

Practice, practice, practice and you will get even better.

Award yourself! On the next page you'll find an award certificate you can photocopy to let the world know you're a **Cartoonist's Apprentice First Class!**

Have you enjoyed this book?

Find out about other books in this series and see sample pages online at

www.123draw.com

Cartoonist's Apprentice First Class

THIS IS TO CERTIFY THAT

_____

HAS SUCCESSFULLY COMPLETED THE "1-2-3 DRAW CARTOON CARS" COURSE.

_____
DATE

Steve Barr
INSTRUCTOR